神道

H. E. DAVEY

SHINTO

MEDITATIONS

FOR REVERING THE EARTH

Stuart D. B. Picken

Foreword by Yukitaka Yamamoto, High Priest of Tsubaki Grand Shrine

STONE BRIDGE PRESS · BERKELEY, CALIFORNIA

Published by
STONE BRIDGE PRESS
P. O. Box 8208, Berkeley, CA 94707
510-524-8732 • sbp@stonebridge.com • www.stonebridge.com

Cover design by Linda Ronan incorporating an image of Itsukushima Shrine, Miyajima, Japan.

Calligraphy on frontispiece: "Shinto" by H. E. Davey.

Misogi exercise on pages 105–12 adapted from *Kami no Michi, The Way of the Kami: The Life and Thought of a Shinto Priest* by Guji Yukitaka Yamamoto, Introduction by Stuart D. B. Picken (Stockton, CA: Tsubaki America Publications, 1987).

Our gratitude to Rev. Koichi Barrish, H. E. Davey, Shunkichi (Yuji) Inokuma, and Peter St. Onge for advice and assistance.

Photographs on pages 13, 17, 20, 97 courtesy Tsubaki Grand Shrine, Japan. Photograph on page 101 courtesy Wago Enten, Hawaii. Photographs on pages 113, 120 courtesy Tsubaki Grand Shrine of America, Washington.

Text © 2002 Stuart D. B. Picken.

First on-demand edition 2020.

Printed in the United States of America.

LIBRARY OF CONGRESS CATALOGING-IN-PUBLICATION DATA
Picken, Stuart D. B.
   Shinto meditations for revering the earth / Stuart D. B.
 Picken; foreword by Yukitaka Yamamoto.
      p. cm.
   ISBN 978-1-880656-66-2
   1. Shinto—Prayer-books and devotions—English. 2.
Nature—Religious aspects—Shinto—Meditations. I. Title.

BL2224.3 .P53 2002
299'.561432—dc21

                                    2002021183

Contents

Foreword

The Human, the Divine, and Great Nature

According to Shinto thinking, human beings are descended from the world of the divine, the world of the *kami*. The cosmic process called Great Nature, the collective reality we call the universe, is honored even by those kami that brought it into being. Within the vast compass of Great Nature, therefore, together, things that exist are given life and thus human beings become able to enjoy the happiness of truth and sincerity. This is the principle that binds heaven and earth, which is called Kannagara, the Way of the Kami. The way known as Kannagara can be understood as the character that lies at the foundation of the existence of all humanity, the principle of mutually cooperative peaceful coexistence.

Modern human civilization, however, has been and is still proceeding on a trajectory of development that seeks to conquer the vast expanses of Great Nature, a pathway that will lead to its own inescapable self-destruction. Human beings henceforth must learn conciliation. The world's religions, their leaders, their

7

doctrines, and their teachings must take the initiative and engage in dialogue that will lead to an initiative to rehabilitate and reestablish the displaced principle of heaven and earth. This must lead to the building of a new order and to a turnabout in thinking that will promote tolerance, generosity, and understanding. This is the meaning of Kannagara, the way of following Great Nature. It is not a religion to be taught, but the source of true and valid religious sentiment.

Human beings, as living bodies, become quite unaware of how impurities that pollute the soul are acquired. They may be descendants of the kami, but they are not kami as such. The soul and the body require constant purification. Through the regular Shinto practice of *misogi* (purification under a waterfall, in a river, or in the sea), human spirituality can be heightened and humanity may be restored to its initial divine, kami nature. Only thus can the human, the divine, and Great Nature be once again brought back into their primal harmony. This is the way toward the cultivation and restoration of human divinity.

This book of meditations gathers common features of natural religion from different faith traditions and shows how they can be used in a Shinto context to revere the earth and cultivate human spirituality. I believe that now is the time for human civilization to unite in achieving this goal. And I believe that Shinto can help show the way.

Yukitaka Yamamoto
96th High Priest of Tsubaki Grand Shrine
The First District Shrine of Ise
Mie Prefecture, Japan

Preface

Does religion puzzle you? An old professor of mine explained this by using the analogy of a tiger—it fascinates you, but you are nevertheless afraid of it. Do you ever feel that you want to belong actively to a group that seeks the cultivation of human spirituality? Do you also become disappointed that, often as not, these groups demand in return that you submit to articles of faith you really don't find "believable"? And doesn't it seem difficult to choose among the wide array of faiths open to you? Do you feel a special reverence for nature and the environment but lack the means to explore this feeling or reference it in your daily life? If the answer to any or all of these is "Yes," then this book is for you.

I would like to talk to you about the most straightforward and basic approach to religion that there is or ever has been. I would like to help awaken you to what religion began as, when nature was the spirit's only guide. Before prophets and gurus, priests and preachers, human beings followed their own inner stirrings, and their religion was natural religion. It was not manmade, artificial, or invented. Its sentiments, beliefs, and responses were drawn from direct communion with the natural. It does not mean that its followers merely worshiped nature, but they did possess a special feeling toward it. They lived within it, and—unlike us today, who are so far from the natural, the authentic, and the immediate—it lived within them.

This religion really was in every sense of the term "prehistoric." It emerged before history was invented to tell us who we are, where we came from, and what we should do with ourselves. It predates the great religions of history. Before the Buddha was born in India, or Jesus of Nazareth preached to the Jews, or Laotzu wrote about the Tao, it was there.

This simple approach to religion that listens to nature, that enriches spirituality, and that restores purity does exist. It has survived in only one modern technological society. It is called *Shinto*, and it lives in modern Japan.

The word Shinto (pronounced like "sheen-toe") is a compound of two Chinese characters, *shin*, which is a kind of generic term referring to the divine, and *do*, which quite simply means "the way." So in short, it refers to the "way of the divine." As its name implies, it is not a teaching but a way, like a well-trodden forest path. It is there for all to see.

But you might protest, "So? Another religion?" To this the answer is "Yes, but with a difference. There is no known or remembered founder. There is no holy book. There are no systematically worked out doctrines, and there is no central or overarching authority." And, there are people who have discovered it without ever having heard the word Shinto and without having visited Japan.

Let me tell you a true story .

I met Mari on a flight from Boston to Prestwick in Scotland. She had been working as a chaplain in an AIDS center in the Bronx in New York City. She had been born in Scotland and had studied Law and Divinity, planning to be a minister in the Church of Scotland. She felt called by her faith, and in obedience went to the United States to the place where she was working at the time I met her.

It was very clear that the work was filling her with sadness and depression simply through exposing her to misery and suffering on a daily basis. I asked her how she dealt with it: prayer perhaps? Then she told me this story. I should preface it by saying that she was of Highland stock, a descendant, as I am, of the ancient Celts, people who lived close to nature.

"I was desperate for a break from the pressures last year," she said, "so I asked for a month's leave and flew back to Scotland. I rented a car, drove north to the island of Skye, and checked into a small hotel that was on the edge of nowhere. It was spring and the life of nature was reviving. I felt a little ray of hope was lighting on me. I went for a climb up the hills, and it being early in the season, there were no other climbers in sight. After pushing my way through a clump of bushes, within a small wooded patch a few hundred feet up, I came on a small pond that was fed by a waterfall."

I watched her eyes begin to sparkle as she came to this point in the narrative. "I felt as though it was inviting me. I am a Scottish woman with all the inhibitions of our Calvinist tradition, but I resisted myself. I peeled off my clothes and plunged in. I swam under the waterfall, naked, and stood there, letting it wash me. I felt that its cold, fresh, and pure waters were cleansing me, restoring me to a purer self, and healing the wounds that the sufferings of life had inflicted. I felt uplifted and left the pond feeling completely renewed. It was as though I had been born again."

She had discovered Shinto without knowing its name and without the help of a teacher.

Then she asked me, almost with uncertainty, "Is that strange?" "No," was my reply. "You have, in that simple experience, discovered what religion was like when nature itself was the guide. You found it by yourself. I found it in Japan. There, it is called Shinto."

I was really moved. It was eloquent confirmation of what I have believed and seen. If Mari could find this experience, so can you or anyone else who wants to find rebirth and restoration in a natural way.

Climbing mountains has been practiced in Japan for countless centuries as a way to find purity. Let's use that metaphor of steps toward the divine—not intellectual or doctrinal leaps of understanding, but progress based on pure, unmediated, and authentic experience, with nature as our teacher and our guide.

I would like to walk with you through the steps of this ascent.

Stuart D. B. Picken
Nagoya, Japan

Shinto and Nature

Everybody needs beauty as well as bread, places to play in and pray in, where nature may heal and give strength to body and soul alike. —JOHN MUIR, *The Yosemite* (1912)

As concerned citizens of the earth, we preserve and protect our natural surroundings. We nurture, conserve, and recycle the resources nature provides us. We do our best to appreciate the unique landscape that encircles us, but we don't usually converse with rocks, give thanks to mountains, or stand praying under the freezing downpour of waterfalls. We are in awe of the beauty, wonder, and power of nature, but we haven't found a way to authentically and meaningfully commune with it. Shinto offers that way to those of us who seek to reestablish the connection between humans and the divine spirit of nature.

In the latter half of the twentieth century, many of us grew increasingly concerned with what was being done to the environment by the intrusion of modern technology. The developments that began with the industrial revolution had given us in the West greater means for the production of food and goods, increasingly faster methods of transportation, and broader distribution of energy and fuel. We humans had utterly transformed the planet for our own comfort and convenience. Battle after battle with nature had been won, but much had been lost. As people became aware of the damage and began to calculate the cost, we recognized that we had placed our own needs above all else, and the victory seemed hollow, empty, and shameful. The waters were poisoned, the air fouled, the land desecrated. We realized that we were about to kill Mother Earth.

Our awareness led us to take action to save our environment, but has it led us to save ourselves? We feel something special for nature as we hike forest paths and stroll beaches, but most of us haven't discovered how to articulate or explore this deep feeling. Even if we witness the spiritual dimension of the natural world, it seems impossible for us to enter into it, to interact with it, to bring its lessons to our lives. In the quote above, John Muir refers to praying in nature, letting it heal and repair us. But how can this be done? The practices of the Shinto tradition nurture the bond between the divinity of nature and the soul of humans. In doing so, Shinto seeks the spiritual unification of ourselves with the elements of our world for the benefit of both.

The Natural Roots of Shinto

Shinto was the communal response of the ancient immigrant dwellers of Japan to the stunning natural environment in which they found themselves. It took hundreds of years before it received a name. In fact, it was not until Buddhism had arrived from China and Korea that the ancient Japanese realized how different their own way of thinking was from that of the high civilizations

The honden is the main worship hall. At Tsubaki Grand Shrine, it is in the classical style of plain, unpainted Japanese cypress with a stylized roof distinguished by ridge posts possibly derived from weights laid on the straw roofs of ancient pit dwellings. Shrine buildings are often razed and rebuilt, preserving the form but renewing the substance.

of the Asian continent. When the way of the Buddha entered Japan in the sixth century it was new, impressive, and initially alien. Unlike the "ancient way," as Shinto was sometimes called, this imported religion had an origin, an originator, and a well-structured set of teachings and traditions. Buddha found enlightenment, became spiritually awake, then set out to spread what he had learned.

Shinto, by contrast, seemed self-evident to its first followers. Wherever they looked, they saw mystery. They confronted it in surging rivers, giant rocks, and pounding waterfalls. They felt it in thundering volcanoes, roaring winds, and the consuming fire of lightning. They sensed it also in the gentler beauty of majestic trees and in the silent dignity of great mountains. They saw it high above in the sun, the moon, and the stars. Before they had discovered how to read and write, they spoke of nature's mysteries as *kami*, that which inspired awe and wonder.

Who were these people? Various studies suggest that they came from as far away as northern Mongolia, central Asia, the Korean peninsula, and the south of Polynesia. They came together and eventually fused into a race that occupied a string of islands stretching from the eastern border of Russia to Taiwan. We do not know exactly who these people were, but we do know that they became the collective spiritual founders of the tradition we call Shinto, the "way of the kami."

There were kami in everything throughout the universe, and anything could be kami. It was a universe pervaded by the divine, an environment in which divine and human were in constant communion, a sacred universe in which the material and the spiritual were inextricably united and where humans and their divinities coexisted. And this is the secret that explains how these early people's mythology was constructed and what it was intended to convey to succeeding generations.

The mythology of ancient Japan has puzzled scholars and lay people alike because it is difficult to fit into any ready-made models. It is neither systematic nor logically consistent. Western mythology is usually approached by scholars and believers seeking personal existential enlightenment or moral guidance—that is, if they take it seriously at all. Mythology gave the Japanese cosmic identity and a sense of descent in a collective rather than individual sense. And it always pointed back to their origins in the "Age of the Kami."

Like all great religions of the world, Shinto mythology does address the origins of life and the universe. The story goes that the kami of birth and the kami of growth emerged from the cosmic chaos of the universe's beginnings and sparked the power of creation underlying the formation of all life. Izanagi and Izanami—primal figures reminiscent of Adam and Eve—descended to the "floating bridge of heaven" and set about populating the land that they themselves had formed by dipping a jeweled spear into the primordial soup that was the planet at the time. Izanami gave birth to the multitude of kami of the earth, but died delivering the last, the kami of fire. Izanagi followed Izanami into the place of death, referred to as "the land of pollution," to retrieve his lover. Izanami refused to leave and ordered Izanagi out by threatening to kill a thousand people a day as long as he remained. Izanagi countered that he would see to it that five hundred more would be born than killed. Izanagi's affirmation expresses the Shinto belief in the power of life over death, creation over destruction, and renewal over decay.

Finally, his efforts to bring back Izanami in vain, Izanagi returned and washed the impurities of the land of pollution from himself in the Tachibana River—a ritual of purification still practiced in Shinto in various forms. While washing himself, the three kami whom Izanagi charged with the rule of the earth miraculously appeared from his eyes and nose. Those kami were the kami of the sun (representing light and energy), the kami of the moon (silence and growth), and the kami of the sea and stars (the rhythms and motion of life). Contrast this to the Hindu "Trinity" (especially the maker of chaos); the kami work in harmony so that the universe is conceived in harmony. The Judeo-Christian

On the right is an ema den, *a location where believers leave prayers written on a small wooden tablet known as an* ema, *which means "picture of a horse." In earlier times horses were presented as gifts to kami. To the left is a small altar where parishioners may offer requests or thanks for prayers answered.*

mythology similarly identifies a defiant and disruptive presence from the beginning that is finally defined as Lucifer, the fallen angel, or Satan, the adversary. For both of these traditions, evil is real and is personified in a quasi-divine form. There is no similar concept in Japanese mythology.

The constant interaction among these three forces provides for the extraordinary power and diversity of nature and also the framework within which humans find themselves. The difference couldn't be any greater between Western traditions, which constantly refer to the human struggle to overcome the natural elements, and those of Shinto, which call for us to harmonize with Daishizen, or "Great Nature."

THE POWER OF GREAT NATURE

While climbing some hills in my native Scotland one recent summer, I experienced nature speaking to me as I am sure it spoke to the Japanese of old. We had just come down a very steep slope that led to an old track we were to follow to the final route of descent. The heights were not vast but steep, slippery, and, above all, bleak—nothing but undulating hills that had probably remained unchanged in form for a million years. Apart from a few sheep, nothing could live there and little could grow except the rough grasses that helped to soften the climb. The sky had been darkening, and there were the rumbles in the distance of that rare occurrence, a summer thunderstorm. I was sure we had adequate time, but the storm struck about an hour sooner than expected.

The rain came first. A few drops took only minutes to become a cascade. The rains on the top of the mountain, landing on the spongy mossy peaks, soon ran down the slopes like small rivers. The path was quickly under inches of water and its outer edge was being washed into a valley on the right hundreds of feet below. The thunder then became louder. Lurid flashes of lightning began zapping the slopes, the hillside, and finally the little track we were trying to follow. After passing almost directly overhead, it began stabbing the track again just behind where we were walking. Each peal of thunder and every streak of lightning felt like heaven growling in anger at those who would challenge its power. After a tense period of around thirty minutes, we finally spotted some rocks that we knew marked the commencement of the descent, and with only two hours before dark, they were a very welcome sight.

I reflected afterward that it is only when people face the power of nature in such a situation, where life is truly at risk, that the meaning of the awesome power of nature comes home to them. Natural disasters may do the same, but fierce storms have most dramatically brought people face to face with the power of the divine throughout the ages. There was the theophany Moses witnessed on Mt. Sinai when he received the Ten Commandments. There was also the equally dramatic storm encountered by the sixteenth-century Reformation leader Martin Luther that led to his religious conversion.

NATURE AS A LIFE FORCE

Going through this experience that began on a beautiful, dry sunny morning, and thinking about this book, I could not help trying to imagine how people of ancient times would reflect on what had happened. In our modern state of mind, we analyze and quantify. We talk of the latent power in such phenomena as lightning. We turn it into electricity and use it for light and heat. But to ancient people, it was the effervescent energy of nature that first impressed them. Its vitality and terrifying power left the indelible impression on their minds of being a life force with its own will and purpose. Thunder was divine, and its highly visible and extremely audible divinity created awe and wonder in the eyes and in the hearts of the beholders. The followers of Shinto called it *kaminari*, "the divinity arriving," and they treated it with respect. They lived in that world in which the divine, nature, and human beings exist together, the world of religious culture, when nature, and nature alone, was the teacher.

Japanese reverence for nature grew out of a sense of living in a divine environment, one that made the development of human society both desirable and possible. Nature was perceived as self-renewing, a cyclical movement of life that should be marked and celebrated at every important juncture. Worship did not focus on some timeless eternal truths that history enshrined in a founding figure or spiritual guru to whom subsequent believers and followers should compare themselves. Instead, countless bearers of wisdom passed on their vision of Great Nature to those who gradually created the rituals and symbols that expressed their perceptions.

The awareness of nature found in Shinto was derived from its ferocious side, but nature has its gentler side as well, and this is where reverence overtakes fear. Thus Shinto speaks of the *nigimitama*, the gentle, harmonious side, and the *aramitama*, the powerful, wilder side of the kami. *Nigimitama* became more important as the Japanese moved from the hunting and gathering stage of social development to the ways of settled agriculture, to the culture of rice. After they had settled into the rhythm of a rice culture, the forces that they already feared and revered were now seen as beneficent sources of all that was needed to grow, protect, and harvest their rice. The fierce lightning that could kill with a blow was also the kami of sheet lightning that heralds the rain needed to grow rice. Kami of water and earth became coworkers in the cultivation of the precious crop. This symbiotic relationship points to the origins and core beliefs of Shinto.

The False Shinto

Sadly, the first image a Westerner may have of Shinto was shaped by the nationalistic propaganda employed by both sides of the Pacific during World War II. State Shinto, as it is called to differentiate itself from the ancient way, hijacked the natural religion of Shinto and pressed it into patriotic service from the beginning of modernization in the Meiji period (1868–1912) to the time leading up to the Pacific War when the militaristic government of Japan was building an empire across China and Southeast Asia. The American government viewed this distortion of Shinto as a cause of Japanese aggression, labeling it "the Great Evil." State Shinto, in reality, lasted less than the seventy years of its official life. Oddly, it was a respectful but misplaced attempt to copy the influence and traditions of Christianity among the imperial powers of Europe.

State Shinto's failure paralleled Japan's surrender. With the dismantling of prewar societal structures by the occupying forces, a natural religion was burdened with a reputation as a system of ultranationalist indoctrination when in reality, as recent studies have shown, the Education Ministry and the Kyoto School of Zen Buddhism were bigger culprits

Close to sixty years after the war, in the new millennium, Shinto has slowly emerged from the gloom of misunderstanding. Apart from a few unenlightened cynics who refuse to believe even the most basic evidence to the contrary, Shinto is returning to its origins and trying again to become what it always was, the spiritual roots of the Japanese people.

This is the Shinto I wish you to find—the Shinto whose true characteristics are caught rather than taught—for this is the

Shinto that can revitalize the natural aspects of human spirituality by teaching us how the world is seen with nature as our guide.

Shinto Symbolism and Ritual

Shinto from Japan is capable of enriching all religion with an awareness of the universal found in prehistorical religious cultures. Since Shinto's source is nature and not doctrines of supernatural revelation, it isn't mutually exclusive to any religious belief. I make comparisons between Western religious traditions and Shinto not to claim its superiority but rather to put Shinto into a context that connects it to all authentic forms of natural human spirituality. As a religion itself, Shinto offers a return to a more elemental, as opposed to elementary, way of viewing our world and ourselves.

The ancient Hebrews' finest insight in the Book of Genesis was "God saw what He had made and He saw that it was good." From ancient India, the *Bhagavad-Gita* declared that "The unreal never is: the Real is never not. This truth indeed has been seen by those who can see the true." The *Tao Te Ching* opens with the sentence "The Tao that can be named is not the true Tao." Goodness and mystery lie at the heart of the universe, and wisdom commences in the recognition of this fact. This opens our minds to a new way of "knowing." It is not knowledge in the intellectual sense, but an internalized knowledge born of the deepest kinds of spiritual experience of which human beings are capable.

Christian traditions also recognize the essential goodness of nature, but we ourselves are not viewed as generously. We are taught that we are born in sin, original sin, and that only Divine grace can save us. Shinto sees things quite differently. The human spirit is born pure and light, but as we grow and experience the world, as we make mistakes and suffer setbacks, the spirit accumulates *tsumi*, impurity. The rituals of Shinto detailed in this book are a way to purify the soul and return it to its original, pristine state. The West embodies the divine in God the Father, and we are His children seeking His good grace. Shinto traces our lineage back to the kami. Purifying our spirits puts us back in touch with the divinity of nature as expressed by our true parents, the kami of the earth.

Shinto's life is found within its rituals. It is less about believing than doing, less about credenda and more about agenda. It is a religion of activity, but activity which is morally and spiritually healthy. It is religion, indeed, as it was before the earth needed to be interpreted and explained to humans. That is why it has survived, and that is what it teaches us. It is not about divine revelation in history. It is about divine revelation within nature.

Shinto lets the symbols of nature become our teachers. Shinto thought sees and expresses nature in a way that makes its meaning self-evident. No explanation is necessary because the meaning is grasped in perceiving the power of the symbol itself. These symbols are also understood in other religions, but their meaning is always put into a context that is derived from revelation or a holy teacher. Shinto lets them speak for themselves.

Shinto rituals involving water do not simply purify human beings. They can also purify an environment. People wash their *genkan* (entranceway) in the morning to prevent misfortune from entering. Little piles of salt may be seen outside restaurants or businesses before they open. Salt is a powerful purifying agent and has the same role of protection. Shinto tends to view misfortune as one of the greatest obstacles to happiness and therefore seeks ways to avoid calamities. These rituals are not the superstitions of an evil-fearing people but are instead acts meant to cleanse the environment literally and metaphorically.

There is also something refreshing about feeling washed and clean, especially if the symbolism of running water suggests that all traces of impurity or dirt are being washed away down the stream to be lost in the sea. This process is suggested and its validity confirmed by nature. It is this that makes a ritual like *misogi*, the purification rite performed under a waterfall, so meaningful. The action and impact of the water has its own suggestive power that, to be fully understood, is best experienced first-hand, as I shall explain later.

If it is to purify effectively, water itself must be clean and pure, fresh and sparkling, which nature suggests is water's proper condition. Of course, artificial and manmade waterways exist that cannot always be kept in such a state. Human commerce inevitably leads to environmental impact of one kind or another. While Shinto images may not solve problems at this level, they help keep alive our strivings for the clean water and clean air associated with the nature that purifies and renews.

Shinto shows us how to purify and to renew all of life in the spirit of the divine once the character of the divine is known. The idea of transformation can apply not only to individual human beings, but also to societies and cultural traditions. Even civilization itself may be renewed. Transformation can also, of course, apply to any religion that is positive in its core and that seeks the well-being of humankind. Religions that do other than that are hardly worthy of the name. The great religions of revelation of the West can seek these transforming powers that are the great contribution of Shinto, the way of the divine. Unlike the religions of revelation, Shinto is not a message from God. It is simply a way by which people can attune themselves to the message of nature, and by that means, seek the divine.

Shinto Meditations as Litanies

The meditations in this book are presented in the form of litanies. A litany is a prayer spoken directly to a god or spirit and usually contains an itemized list of observations and hoped-for blessings. The concept, practice, and use of litanies may seem out of place in a natural religion such as Shinto, but consider litanies in Christian tradition, which were designed not only to bond followers to the Church but also to address private devotion or to appease God after natural disasters. Litanies could be prayers for the ill to recover or for the spiritually lost to find their way. Roman Catholics end their "Kyrie Eleison" litany with the phrase "Save us, restore us again, O Lord, by Thy mercy." While the relationship between the petitioners and the petitioned is far different in the Cathedral than in Great Nature, the longing for a healing of the soul is not.

The litanies presented hereafter are not translations but were prepared in English especially for this book. Based on Shinto concepts, they are built around Shinto *norito* ("invocations of the divine") and blended with the more general elements of religious litanies found worldwide. This is not to deny their Shinto heritage, but rather to demonstrate the universality of Shinto inspiration. From the essence of these elements, I tried to tap the deepest spiritual meaning and render it in a form that can be used by individuals or groups for worship or meditation. The purpose is to arouse and cultivate a genuine spirit of reverence for Great Nature, the cosmic content of all forms of existence, by awakening the mind and connecting it to the cosmos in all its majesty and mystery.

The liturgy is an awakening of the cosmic that lives within humanity. It is also an awakening of the human toward the cosmic, enriching responsibility through reverence. In the shrine of Daishizen, the Church of Great Nature, we can become permeated by the pure religion of nature so that we may learn to revere Creation, the Created, and the Creative Force.

I assume that you've picked up this book and read this far because you already have a deep respect for nature but are seeking some more meaningful way to address it, revere it, and allow it to live within you. I hope that the meditations I've prepared for this book provide some understanding and framework for you to commune with the divine found through nature's guidance.

A Guide to Using the Meditations

There are eight litanies for meditation, two for each season. Each litany addresses an element of nature and spiritually ascends through seven stages of awareness, from observation and awakening to celebration. Although clearly structured, each meditation has been designed to be flexible in its use. You can recite these invocations by yourself in solitary meditation or in a worship group (where one person will read as "leader"), indoors or, better, outside in the Cathedral of Great Nature.

The language used in these meditations may seem liturgical or ritualistic—perhaps a bit old-fashioned even—but it is designed to be unfamiliar and thus help you experience the words and sensations with fresh reverence. Also, in Japanese culture, certain words are thought to have *kotodama*, meaning "word-soul." The power of these words enriches and strengthens the invocation. To retain a few of these Japanese words in the meditations may add depth to the experience. Speaking and declaiming the words aloud will help activate your awareness, and perhaps even alert the kami to your presence!

The seven stages of ascent from awakening to celebration can be understood as follows.

1. OBSERVATION (KANNAGARA)

大自然 Look at nature, looking beyond either its beauty or the scars caused by human activity. Ponder anew the mystery of creation, growth, and sustenance, as well as nature's capacity to heal and renew. Wonder at the infinity of the cosmos, the myriad of stars and planets, and the unique position of the earth that permits the delicate balance for life to exist. Consciousness of the great flow of the cosmos is awareness of *kannagara*, the movement of the divine within us and around us. Observation with an open mind helps to purify our vision.

Before reading or using these litanies, take time to look at and ponder some of the simple things of life that are often passed over amid the rush and turmoil of modern civilization.

Look at a tree—think about the meaning of growth and development. Consider how this tree constitutes the essence of nature and her processes.

Look at a mountain—think of its age and endurance. Compare our brief lifespan to its seeming eternity.

Look at a flowing river—think of the centuries of motion and movement.

Look at the ocean—think of the deep and mysterious source of life, its eons of ebb and flow, and its beauty and power.

Look at a great rock—ponder its strength and majesty, its usefulness as a home for the birds, a shade in the heat, and a landmark to the lost.

Look at the grass—try to understand the ultimate mystery, the mystery of growth that lies within the seed.

In any one of these elements lies a gateway to understanding the divine as it is around you. This exercise is a first step toward awakening the soul to the unity and universality of all religious truth as Shinto helps us see it.

2. INVOCATION (DAISHIZEN)

惟神 Speak to nature as you would to a friend. Think of the age before creation, when there was only darkness and silence. Then imagine the process unfolding as light dawned and creation began, progressing toward self-fulfillment in the divine visible to those who can perceive it in the natural order. Ask nature to teach you. The Shinto *norito* all contain the invocation:

> *Amatsu kami, Kunitsu kami, yao yorozu no kami . . .*
> (kami of heaven, kami of earth, great myriad of kami . . .)

3. INSPIRATION (KAMI)

産霊 Try to feel gratitude that you are a part of this cosmos that is alive with signs of divine presence. "In-spire" means literally "breathing into," and what we should seek is the kami breathing something into us, filling us with it. This should lead to the awakening or stirring of the soul, the point at which receptivity becomes greatest.

4. PURIFICATION (HARAI)

鎮魂 Grateful awareness of the divine leads to the purification of the soul by restoring the ability to perceive the divine in all of one's surroundings. This is one of the greatest gifts of the Shinto tradition—namely, the restoration of the capacity to see "the good," as it might be stated in Western terms, where it is not at once visible. During this section of the meditation we recite a prayer, the *Rokkon-shojo* ("Six-Root Purification"), that our five senses and our minds be kept pure.

A famous teacher was walking with his disciples. They passed the remains of a dead dog, and one disciple passed a remark at the sight. The teacher stopped, looked at the remains, and said softly, "But it had beautiful teeth." He could see beauty woven

32

in the midst of decay and deformity. It is from this way of seeing that true hope can spring in life and in the world.

5. MEDITATION (CHINKON)

祓 All major acts of purification must be followed by meditation, when the soul calms down after reaching a spiritual height, however modest. The soul must be calmed so that its achievement can be felt and the heightened awareness of the divine can be permitted to flow throughout the entire human being. *Chinkon* can take many forms and is performed differently in different shrines' traditions, but it is designed as an activity to link the spiritual peak experiences with the remainder of life for its greater enrichment.

6. RELATION (MUSUBI)

神 The term *musubi* in Shinto means relation in a practical way and has several dimensions. There is the relation between ourselves and our origin. This is the communion between Great Nature and our most inner and natural selves. This can make possible the renewal of external relations, in which people, kami, and community find new life.

Musubi is a mutual bond of relation that makes growth possible. The fertilization of the seed of understanding is achieved by the growth of the imagination through living relation.

7. CELEBRATION (MATSURI)

祭 The final stage celebrates the human communion with the divine that gives life energy and meaning. The deepest expression of this communion is the freedom it affords us to become children of the cosmos who can approach the source of creativity, without the mediation of religion or science, to know its friendship and care. Through this, the world becomes like a mandala, a cosmogram that sets forth truth, understanding, authentic experience, and the healing power of life itself.

SPRING

HARU
SPRING

Earth

Mother Earth in Religious Thought

The importance of soil and earth becomes obscured or forgotten by those whose natural environment is buildings of concrete and steel, asphalt roads and subway tunnels, bus and truck fumes, and palls of gray, sticky mist that choke the nose and leave black marks on shirt cuffs and collars. The dust and the dirt, far from being nature, become polluting objects that cause allergies and asthma, that dim the vision, block the ears, or obscure the senses of taste and smell. So physical and spiritual purification alike are needed in order to see what earth actually is.

Before industry covered the landscape and the black mills and their smokestacks began to arise, the expression "Mother Earth" was used in contrast to the image of the Heavenly Father in the Western tradition. Most cultures refer to their homeland as the Motherland, symbolizing the female, the earth, and its endless capacity to bring forth new life.

Earth in Shinto

In Shinto rituals, earth is the most basic of the elements. Earth is celebrated in all its fairness and beauty and in its power to feed and support life through growth and development.

Earth and the kami who belong to it are revered and respected. In the ceremony of ground-breaking and purification—called *jichinsai*—those who plan a new building venture or a construction project that involves disturbing earth seek the cooperation and goodwill of the kami who have influence upon that land or who are associated with it. This ceremony can be viewed in many ways. The cynical may call it fetishism or superstition. But it can also be viewed as a primal, unself-conscious, ancient, and symbolic way of asking a very important twenty-first-century question, namely, "Can human beings cooperate with the earth?"

The worlds of the sociosphere and the biosphere seem very far apart. Can they meet? The answer of Shinto is quite emphatically that they can, they do, and they must continue to meet. Earth grows food as well as provides human beings with the place for homes and buildings. Respect is an attitude that human beings must relearn if forgotten or deepen where it already exists.

The Kami of Earth

In Shinto, there are many kami of earth. Sarutahiko Okami (Saru-tahiko-no-Okami) is the head of all the kami of earth and the pioneering kami guiding and directing rice planting and civilization. Acknowledgment of the existence of these kami represents a mythological way of expressing the awareness of the forces and powers within earth that relate to growth and fertility and without which life cannot be sustained and growth cannot take place. To a better human relationship with the kami of earth, this litany is directed.

The Litany of Earth

OBSERVATION: KANNAGARA

Leader   Think of how human beings first experienced earth bringing forth her fruits

Think of how earth was conceived of as a mother and revered for her fertility, her abundant gifts, and her ability to nurture and support life

Think of the seasons as they flow by, the yellow and green of spring in all its newness and freshness

Think of the mystery of the seed, how life is contained within it, and its creative growth

All   Our senses have been dulled and dimmed, and we see earth not as the environment of our life, but as a tool to be used

Our senses are blind to its mystery and meaning

Our senses need the purification that will enable us to see nature as our teacher and guide

INVOCATION: DAISHIZEN

Leader Divine beings, kami

Head kami of earth, Sarutahiko Okami—great and glorious—

Hear us!

All Great Mother Earth, speak to us and teach us your wisdom

In opening ourselves to nature, in seeking its purification, and in hearing what it has to teach us, may we find enlightenment as we share in the fusion of ourselves with the universe that brings us back to the divine found within the human

INSPIRATION: KAMI

Leader Speak to us of the flow of life as growth and not as completion, not as alpha and omega, but as the beginning that never ends and the end that never ceases—the seed that germinates and sprouts new life that in turn grows and falls and leaves the seed to begin its journey again

Teach us the meaning of the seed, the source of creativity, and the movement of life

Speak to us of the meaning of germination, growth, purification, and the communion of elements within the process of becoming eternally new

Show us the fusion of the maternal and paternal forms of the divine that completes our sense of the life of the cosmos

All   Teach us the meaning of purity, brightness, and the uprightness of the soul

Teach us how to return to our higher origins

Teach us the power of purification

PURIFICATION: HARAI

Leader   Let us repeat the words of the *Rokkon-shojo* with careful minds

All   Although the impure and polluted appears before my eyes, I will not let it blind me

Although it strikes my ears, I will not let it make me deaf

Although my nose senses it, I will not let it deform my soul

Although it enters my mouth, I will not let it destroy my taste for life

Although it touches my body, I will not let it cling to me

Although I may even desire it, I will not let that desire dwell within me

[Pause in silence]

Purified, we become free

Purified, our eyes are opened to the beauty and glory of nature

Purified, our ears can hear the harmony of the spheres even amid the discord of life

Purified, our sense of fragrance and spirituality is heightened

Purified, our taste can savor the subtle richness of life

Purified, our hands can touch the world in its strength and delicacy

Purified, our minds see and grasp the world as it is

Through these means, we will magnify the purity of our spirits and seek the divine within the human

MEDITATION: CHINKON

Leader   Think on these things

The earth that never dies, may it continue to support human life

Earth as a form changeless yet ever-changing that can grant us the power of renewal

The divine within the cosmos and the divine within us

All   Those who have eyes that wish to see, may they see

Those who have spirits they seek to stir, may they feel stirred

Those who have lives to purify, may they feel purified

RELATION: MUSUBI

Leader Think of ourselves as purified and restored to our potential

Think of us once again bound to nature and to the world around us in new and meaningful divine relation

Think of us as truly part of Great Nature

All The power and purifying energy of nature, we will revere

The kami of heaven and earth, we will revere

CELEBRATION: MATSURI

Leader Be thankful and be filled with the joy of life

Be thankful for what earth has taught you about life

Celebrate your purification

Rejoice in your enlightenment

All We sing out our gratitude to the kami of heaven and earth

We celebrate in communion with the kami of heaven and earth and with those around us

Waterfalls

The Majesty of the Falls

Shinto grew and developed from the earliest times of Japanese civilization within the munificent and rich bounties of nature that had been conferred upon the Japanese islands. Among the first things to strike the ancient Japanese with wonder and awe were the great waterfalls shaped by the steep rising slopes of Japan's mountains. The famous ones can drop hundreds of feet into open ravines with a majesty and power that was clearly compelling to those who came to view them as objects of contemplative reverence.

This litany seeks to provide a means to bring human life and the falls into a communion from which purification and renewal may come.

The Litany of the Waterfall

OBSERVATION: KANNAGARA

Leader Let us consider the nature of the divine, Nature the Mother and Nature the Father, the softness and hardness of water

Let us think of the self-disclosure of the divine in the providence and power of nature

Let us think of the waterfall as a concentration of beauty, power, and energy united in endlessly renewing flow

All Our senses have been dulled and dimmed, and we see nature not as the environment of our life but as a tool to be used

Our senses are blind to its mystery and meaning

Our senses need the purification that will enable us to see nature as our teacher and guide

INVOCATION: DAISHIZEN

Leader In the flow of the falls, all purity is removed and washed away

The flow of life carries away those things that we neither need nor want

All Great Falls, speak to us and teach us your wisdom

In opening ourselves to nature, in seeking its purification, and in hearing what it has to teach us, may we find enlightenment as we share in the fusion of ourselves with the universe that brings us back to the divine that is within the human

INSPIRATION: KAMI

Leader   Speak to us of the flow of life as growth and not as completion, not as alpha and omega, but as the beginning that never ends and the end that never ceases—the trickle of drops that grow into an ocean

Speak to us of the meaning of change, purification, and the communion of elements within the process of becoming eternally new

All   Teach us the meaning of purity, brightness, and the uprightness of the soul

Teach us how to return to our higher origins

Teach us the power of purification

PURIFICATION: HARAI

Leader   Let us repeat the words of the *Rokkon-shojo* with careful minds

All   Although the impure and polluted appears before my eyes, I will not let it blind me

Although it strikes my ears, I will not let it make me deaf

Although my nose senses it, I will not let it deform my soul

Although it enters my mouth, I will not let it destroy my taste for life

Although it touches my body, I will not let it cling to me

Although I may even desire it, I will not let that desire dwell within me

[Pause in silence]

Purified, we become free

Purified, our eyes are opened to the beauty and glory of nature

Purified, our ears can hear the harmony of the spheres even amid the discord of life

Purified, our sense of fragrance and spirituality is heightened

Purified, our taste can savor the subtle richness of life

Purified, our hands can touch the world in its strength and delicacy

Purified, our minds see and grasp the world as it is

Through these means, we will magnify the purity of our spirits and seek the divine within the human

MEDITATION: CHINKON

Leader   Think on these things

The flow that never ceases, the divine that never dies

The form changeless yet ever-changing that can grant us the power of renewal

The divine within the cosmos and the divine within us

All   Those who have eyes that wish to see, may they see

Those who have spirits they seek to stir, may they feel stirred

Those who have lives to purify, may they feel purified

RELATION: MUSUBI

Leader   Think of ourselves as purified and restored to our potential

Think of us once again bound to nature and to the world around us in new and meaningful divine relation

Think of us as truly part of Great Nature

All   The power and purifying energy of nature, we will revere

The kami of heaven and earth, we will revere

CELEBRATION: MATSURI

Leader   Be thankful and be filled with the joy of life

Be thankful for what the falls has taught you about life

Celebrate your purification

Rejoice in your enlightenment

All   We sing out our gratitude to the kami of heaven and earth

We celebrate in communion with the kami of heaven and earth and with those around us

SUMMER

NATSU

SUMMER

Rivers

Rivers in Religious Thought

Flowing water and purification have a close relationship in Shinto. Rivers are used for purification in the same way as waterfalls, and both shape the common symbolic meaning in natural religion of being a source and a means of purification. Both the Hebrew ritual of the Bath of Purity and the Christian sacrament of Baptism were designed to initiate converts by taking advantage of this natural meaning. John the Baptist first gave the ritual a moral dimension in the West. The earliest rituals were performed in rivers until Christianity spread to places that made the use of rivers impossible. Sprinkled water replaced rivers, and, as is often the case with developed religious systems, the emphasis moved away from the idea of purification to the idea of something doctrinal rather than natural.

Shinto, Rivers, and Purification

The Shinto idea of purification contrasts with the strong moral overtones of the Western religious tradition. When bad things happen to good people, Western religion has only two answers. One is moral self-scrutiny, a search for reasons that could have caused the problem, such as punishment for individual misbehavior. If this fails, people are asked to accept the mystery of the theodicy, of why a good God should create evil in the world as an insoluble mystery, as a schooling of character, or as something for which compensation will be paid after death. Comforting as those explanations may be to some people, or even philosophically satisfying to others, they do not say a great deal about how people should respond immediately in the face of disaster, or how they should cope with such events.

Purification as Therapy

Psychologists say that people should neither dwell unnecessarily on nor blame themselves for events outside their control. They should look outward, not inward, and get on with life. This is precisely where ritual purification in Shinto takes on its fullest meaning. It is not a speculative solution to a metaphysical problem. It is a practical step in the face of what might be a paralyzing crisis. Purification in Shinto lifts the burden from the shoulders of the individual and washes it away. "Cut your losses, forget what can be forgotten, take a positive view of life, and just begin again." It is a healthy, extroverted solution to unhealthy, introverted thinking. It is a meaningful act of cosmic absolution from things done to the spirit seeking the release of purification.

The Litany of the River

OBSERVATION: KANNAGARA

Leader   Think of what water by its very nature teaches us

To purify effectively, water itself must be clean, pure, and fresh

Think of the idea of the current, of the endless flow of the river into the seas

Identity amid impermanence is what gives a river its name

In the depth and width, the river reminds us of the difficult expanses of life that must be traversed

Think also of the golden rays and blue skies of summer, its glowing sun and its health-giving warmth and brightness reflected in the sparkling water of the river

Let us think of the self-disclosure of the divine in the providence and power of nature

Let us think of the river bearing away our impurities

All   Our senses have been dulled and dimmed, and we see nature not as the environment of our life, but as a tool to be used

Our senses are blind to its mystery and meaning

Our senses need the purification that will enable us to see nature as our teacher and guide

INVOCATION: DAISHIZEN

Leader   In the flow of the river, all impurity is removed and washed away

The flow of life carries away those things that we neither need nor want

All   Great River, speak to us and teach us your wisdom

In opening ourselves to nature, in seeking its purification, and in hearing what it has to teach us, may we find enlightenment as we share in the fusion of ourselves with the universe that brings us back to the divine that is within the human

INSPIRATION: KAMI

Leader   Speak to us of the flow of life as growth and not as completion, not as alpha and omega, but as the beginning that never ends and the end that never ceases—the trickle of drops that grow into an ocean

Speak to us of the meaning of change, purification, and the communion of elements within the process of becoming eternally new

All   Teach us the meaning of purity, brightness, and the uprightness of the soul

Teach us how to return to our higher origins

Teach us the power of purification

PURIFICATION: HARAI

Leader Let us repeat the words of the *Rokkon-shojo* with careful minds

All Although the impure and polluted appears before my eyes, I will not let it blind me

Although it strikes my ears, I will not let it make me deaf

Although my nose senses it, I will not let it deform my soul

Although it enters my mouth, I will not let it destroy my taste for life

Although it touches my body, I will not let it cling to me

Although I may even desire it, I will not let that desire dwell within me

[Pause in silence]

Purified, we become free

Purified, our eyes are opened to the beauty and glory of nature

Purified, our ears can hear the harmony of the spheres even amid the discord of life

Purified, our sense of fragrance and spirituality is heightened

Purified, our taste can savor the subtle richness of life

Purified, our hands can touch the world in its strength and delicacy

Purified, our minds see and grasp the world as it is

Through these means, we will magnify the purity of our spirits and seek the divine within the human

MEDITATION: CHINKON

Leader   Think on these things

The flow that never ceases, the divine that never dies

The form changeless yet ever-changing that can grant us the power of renewal

The divine within the cosmos and the divine within us

All   Those who have eyes that wish to see, may they see

Those who have spirits they seek to stir, may they feel stirred

Those who have lives to purify, may they feel purified

RELATION: MUSUBI

Leader   Think of ourselves as purified and restored to our potential

Think of us once again bound to nature and to the world around us in new and meaningful divine relation

Think of us as truly part of Great Nature

All   The power and purifying energy of nature, we will revere

The kami of heaven and earth, we will revere

CELEBRATION: MATSURI

Leader   Be thankful and be filled with the joy of life

Be thankful for what the river has taught you about life

Celebrate your purification

Rejoice in your enlightenment

All   We sing out our gratitude to the kami of heaven and earth

We celebrate in communion with the kami of heaven and earth and with those around us

Stones

The Stone as a Religious Symbol

Stones and rocks speak of solidarity, strength, endurance, and protection. In the Judeo-Christian tradition, the oft-sung "Rock of Ages" is perhaps one of the best known symbols of that idea. Jacob slept in the desert using a rock for a pillow he dreamed of before reaching heaven. The rock became a point of contact between earth and heaven, between the human and the divine.

Druid Rocks and Rituals

In ancient Celtic religious traditions, rocks were featured as places where the Druids celebrated the great rituals in honor of the sun. Stones had a power of their own to concentrate energy, to convey meaning, to focus activity, and to transmit authority. There was the Dallan, the Stone of Destiny, thought to be a Druid monument that was part of the sacred sites around the court of Tara, the ancient capital of the Celts. The other great Stone of Destiny used to sit under the throne in Westminster Abbey in London and is now located in Edinburgh Castle. It was probably a coronation stone that later became the stone upon which the kings of Scotland and Ireland received their authority once they had sat upon it. Stones like it are found in different parts of the old Celtic domains in Europe.

Stones in Shinto

As in other cultural traditions, some of the oldest Shinto artifacts remaining in use for religious purposes are stones, some dating back probably 3,000 years. In Shinto, a stone that radiates great beauty, dignity, and elegance and that commands the worshipers' spirits may be adorned with a sacred rope and revered. Stones and rocks used in Japanese gardens often make observers catch their breath. The manner in which they are placed to show their natural beauty at its best, surrounded only by gravel, has long been a device used to stimulate the imagination to contemplate the eternal and the mysterious. However, it is in their natural environmental setting that the power of great stones is best seen.

The Litany of the Stone

OBSERVATION: KANNAGARA

Leader   Let us consider the nature of the divine, Nature the Mother and Nature the Father, the hardness of the stone and the gentle earth in which it is set

Let us think of the self-disclosure of the divine in the providence and power of nature

Let us think of the rocks and stones as a concentration of beauty, power, and energy united in strength and endurance

All   Our senses have been dulled and dimmed, and we see nature not as the environment of our life, but as a tool to be used

Our senses are blind to its mystery and meaning

Our senses need the purification that will enable us to see nature as our teacher and guide

INVOCATION: DAISHIZEN

Leader   Stones speak to us of endurance, strength, power, and mass

Focus upon the image of a stone that speaks to you of the divine

The flow of life carries away those things that we neither need nor want

All   Great Stones, speak to us and teach us your wisdom

In opening ourselves to nature, in seeking its purification, and in hearing what it has to teach us, may we find enlightenment as we share in the fusion of ourselves with the universe that brings us back to the divine that is within the human

We seek the meaning of strength, power, and the endurance of eternity

INSPIRATION: KAMI

Leader   Speak to us of the strength and power of life as endurance and continuity, not as alpha and omega, but as the beginning that never ends and the end that never ceases—the eternal cosmic process

Speak to us of the meaning of change, purification, and the communion of elements within the process of becoming eternally new

All   Teach us the meaning of purity, brightness, and the uprightness of the soul that enables us to perceive the divinity within the stone

Teach us how to return to our higher origins

Teach us the power of purification

PURIFICATION: HARAI

Leader   Let us repeat the words of the *Rokkon-shojo* with careful minds

All   Although the impure and polluted appears before my eyes, I will not let it blind me

Although it strikes my ears, I will not let it make me deaf

Although my nose senses it, I will not let it deform my soul

Although it enters my mouth, I will not let it destroy my taste for life

Although it touches my body, I will not let it cling to me

Although I may even desire it, I will not let that desire dwell within me

[Pause in silence]

Purified, we become free

Purified, our eyes are opened to the beauty and glory of nature

Purified, our ears can hear the harmony of the spheres even amid the discord of life

Purified, our sense of fragrance and spirituality is heightened

Purified, our taste can savor the subtle richness of life

Purified, our hands can touch the world in its strength and delicacy

Purified, our minds see and grasp the world as it is

Through these means, we will magnify the purity of our spirits and seek the divine within the human

MEDITATION: CHINKON

Leader   Think on these things

Look at a great stone and ponder its strength and majesty

A home for birds

A shade in the heat

A landmark to the lost

Let us learn from the great stones

Let the identity that endures change and transition give confidence to our changing

All   Those who have eyes that wish to see, may they see

Those who have spirits they seek to stir, may they feel stirred

Those who have lives to purify, may they feel purified

RELATION: MUSUBI

Leader   Think of ourselves as purified and restored to our potential

Think of us once again bound to nature and to the world around us in new and meaningful divine relation

Think of us as truly part of Great Nature

All   The power and purifying energy of nature, we will revere

The kami of heaven and earth, we will revere

CELEBRATION: MATSURI

Leader Be thankful and be filled with the joy of life

Be thankful for what the rocks and stones have taught you about life

Celebrate your purification

Rejoice in your enlightenment

All We sing out our gratitude to the kami of heaven and earth

We celebrate in communion with the kami of heaven and earth and with those around us

AUTUMN

AKI
AUTUMN

Trees

Trees and the Sacred

As a graduate student, I recollect the Professor of Divinity reading the following passage from the Hebrew philosopher Martin Buber (1878–1965) for discussion in a seminar:

> I consider a tree.
>
> I can look at it as a picture: stiff column in a shock of light, or a splash of green shot with the delicate blue and silver of the background.
>
> I can perceive it as movement: flowing veins on clinging pith, suck of the roots, breathing of the leaves, ceaseless commerce with earth and air—and the obscure growth itself. I can classify it in a species and study it as a type in its structure and mode of life. . . .
>
> It can, however, come about, if I have both will and grace, that in considering the tree I become bound up in relation to it. The

tree is no longer It. I have been seized by the power of exclusive-
ness. . . .

   Everything belonging to the tree is in this: its form and struc-
ture, its colors and chemical composition, its intercourse with
the elements and with the stars, are all present in a single whole.
. . . Let no attempt be made to sap the strength from the meaning of relation: relation is mutual. [*I and Thou*, trans. Ronald Gregor
Smith (Edinburgh: T. and T. Clark, 1937), pp. 7–8]

I remember the sound of supercilious, muffled laughter
that greeted the reading of the passage, and yet it seems now so
sensible and sympathetic. Christian orthodoxy still wishes to revere the Creator but not Creation.

Trees in Shinto

In Shinto a tree may be a kami (*shinboku*) around whose wide
trunk a thick twisted rope, a *shimenawa*, is tied to show its sacred
status. There are too many famous shinboku throughout Japan to
detail. Nearly every village or town has one in the precincts of its
largest shrine. Some are famous because of historical incidents
that happened to them and others simply because of their vener-
able age.

   In Shinto rituals, the kami descend upon evergreens, prin-
cipally the *sakaki*, unique to Japan and related to the camellia. It
was in the forests and groves of Japan that the sense of sacred
places found its origin. Many of these sites subsequently became
shrines.

   In these places we can contemplate not only our human
dependence upon the tree for continued life but also the tree as a

symbol of the creative and protective powers of nature. The litany here seeks to draw attention to this.

The Litany of the Tree

OBSERVATION: KANNAGARA

Leader   Trees teach us about growth

They also stand for shelter

They are, like water, living organisms

Ponder the meaning of growth and development

Think of how we know nature through our senses, our eyes, our taste, our sense of smell and touch, our awareness and deep intuitions

Let us think of the self-disclosure of the divine in the providence and power of nature

Let us think of the trees as expressions of beauty, power, and energy united in endless renewal

All   Our senses have been dulled and dimmed, and we see nature not as the environment of our life, but as a tool to be used, trees for building and burning

Our senses are blind to its mystery and meaning

Our senses need the purification that will enable us to see nature as our teacher and guide

INVOCATION: DAISHIZEN

Leader In the life of a tree, we may see a microcosm of the universe

All Great Trees, speak to us and teach us your wisdom

In opening ourselves to nature, in seeking its purification, and in hearing what it has to teach us, may we find enlightenment as we share in the fusion of ourselves with the universe that brings us back to the divine that is within the human

INSPIRATION: KAMI

Leader Speak to us of the flow of life as growth and not as completion, not as alpha and omega, but as the beginning that never ends and the end that never ceases—like the acorn that grows into the mighty oak

Speak to us of the meaning of change, purification, and the communion of elements within the process of becoming eternally new

All Teach us the meaning of purity, brightness, and the uprightness of the soul

Teach us how to return to our higher origins

Teach us the power of purification

PURIFICATION: HARAI

Leader Let us repeat the words of the *Rokkon-shojo* with careful minds

All Although the impure and polluted appears before my eyes, I will not let it blind me

Although it strikes my ears, I will not let it make me deaf

Although my nose senses it, I will not let it deform my soul

Although it enters my mouth, I will not let it destroy my taste for life

Although it touches my body, I will not let it cling to me

Although I may even desire it, I will not let that desire dwell within me

[Pause in silence]

Purified, we become free

Purified, our eyes are opened to the beauty and glory of nature

Purified, our ears can hear the harmony of the spheres even amid the discord of life

Purified, our sense of fragrance and spirituality is heightened

Purified, our taste can savor the subtle richness of life

Purified, our hands can touch the world in its strength and delicacy

Purified, our minds see and grasp the world as it is

Through these means, we will magnify the purity of our spirits and seek the divine within the human

MEDITATION: CHINKON

Leader   Think of trees teaching us the steadiness of growth and of the time required for greatness to develop

Ponder why weeds grow faster than flowers, and why bushes grow faster than trees

Weeds wither in the heat of the sun

Trees grow and give shade

Trees are forms of the changeless yet ever-changing that can teach us the power of renewal

The divine within the cosmos and the divine within us

All   Those who have eyes that wish to see, may they see

Those who have spirits they seek to stir, may they feel stirred

Those who have lives to purify, may they feel purified

RELATION: MUSUBI

Leader   Think of ourselves as purified and restored to our potential

Think of us once again bound to nature and to the world around us in new and meaningful divine relation

Think of us as truly part of Great Nature

All The power and purifying energy of nature, we will revere

The kami of heaven and earth, we will revere

CELEBRATION: MATSURI

Leader Be thankful and be filled with the joy of life

Be thankful for what the tree has taught you about life

Celebrate your purification

Rejoice in your enlightenment

All We sing out our gratitude to the kami of heaven and earth

We celebrate in communion with the kami of heaven and earth and with those around us

Wind & Lightning

Wind as Spirit

In the Hebrew tradition, the wind moved across the face of the waters and brought Creation into being. Symbolized frequently by wind, the breath of God as the spirit of creative energy became a fundamental concept of Hebrew religion as a way of speaking indirectly of the presence of the divine.

In the Christian era, the gift of the Holy Spirit to the church at Pentecost was marked by the sound of a mighty rushing wind. Indeed, manifestations of the divine are often spoken of as accompanied by the power of the wind. Nature provides yet another self-evident symbol of the divine, namely energy that can be felt but not seen. For this reason, perhaps, wind has retained religious symbolic significance.

In Indian, Chinese, and esoteric Buddhist cultures, lightning became the symbol of the cosmic power of enlightenment. In the Japanese tradition of Shingon, a lightning bolt is in the hand of Buddha's agent Fudo-myoo, giving him the power to cast out impurity and evil wherever they exist. The mountain ascetics of Shinto and Buddhism who seek the way of enlightenment through discipline invoke the protection of Fudo-myoo.

Wind and Lightning in Shinto

Lightning and wind have ambiguous powers and influence. Lightning is marked by great white flashes and rocking blasts of sound, and on a summer day can appear as if to leap forth from suddenly gathered, darkened masses of clouds. From lightning comes powerful energy and from that ravaging fires. As human civilization has developed we have learned to harness and produce energies very much like lightning, but still do we give it respect and indicate its generative sources like power plants and batteries with signs of danger and warning.

Wind may be a gentle, soothing breeze or a calamitous hurricane or twisting tornado. Wind sweeps in invisibly and yet causes things in our world to stir and rustle. And while we can harness the wind, we can neither slow nor contain it.

Our awareness of wind and lightning's ambiguous nature is heightened by the experience of civilization and the occasional impact of nature's wilder face upon it. The *norito* invocations of Shinto do not pretend to control these. They seek simply to purify people from those things that the kami find distressing while at the same time expressing appreciation to the elements for the positive gifts they confer upon life through winds, lightning, and rain. This litany tries to express and unite these positive themes.

The Litany of Wind & Lightning

OBSERVATION: KANNAGARA

Leader   The wind is not seen, it is felt

Let us consider the nature of the divine, Nature the Mother and Nature the Father, the invisible powers that keep the world in place

Let us think of the self-disclosure of the divine in the providence and power of nature

Let us think of the concentration of beauty, power, and energy united in wind and lightning

All   Our senses have been dulled and dimmed, and we see nature not as the environment of our life, but as a tool to be used

Our senses are blind to its mystery and meaning

Our senses need the purification that will enable us to see nature as our teacher and guide

INVOCATION: DAISHIZEN

Leader   The wind and the lightning speak to us of the visible and invisible forces that touch the physical life of the environment, sometimes to bless and sometimes to bring chaos

Lightning can make rice grow

Lightning can set a forest on fire

All Great Wind and Lightning, speak to us and teach us your wisdom

In opening ourselves to nature, in seeking its purification, and in hearing what it has to teach us, may we find enlightenment as we share in the fusion of ourselves with the universe that brings us back to the divine that is within the human

INSPIRATION: KAMI

Leader Speak to us of the flow of life as growth and not as completion, not as alpha and omega, but as the beginning that never ends and the end that never ceases—the breath that is never exhausted

Speak to us of the meaning of change, purification, and the communion of elements within the process of becoming eternally new

All Teach us the meaning of purity, brightness, and the uprightness of the soul

Teach us how to return to our higher origins

Teach us the power of purification

PURIFICATION: HARAI

Leader Let us repeat the words of the *Rokkon-shojo* with careful minds

All   Although the impure and polluted appears before my eyes, I will not let it blind me

Although it strikes my ears, I will not let it make me deaf

Although my nose senses it, I will not let it deform my soul

Although it enters my mouth, I will not let it destroy my taste for life

Although it touches my body, I will not let it cling to me

Although I may even desire it, I will not let that desire dwell within me

[Pause in silence]

Purified, we become free

Purified, our eyes are opened to the beauty and glory of nature

Purified, our ears can hear the harmony of the spheres even amid the discord of life

Purified, our sense of fragrance and spirituality is heightened

Purified, our taste can savor the subtle richness of life

Purified, our hands can touch the world in its strength and delicacy

Purified, our minds see and grasp the world as it is

Through these means, we will magnify the purity of our spirits and seek the divine within the human

MEDITATION: CHINKON

Leader   Think on these things

The wind that is not seen can shift a desert

The lightning bolt can split a rock asunder

It reminds us of how to seek truth directly and decisively

The divine within the cosmos and the divine within us

All   Those who have eyes that wish to see, may they see

Those who have spirits they seek to stir, may they feel stirred

Those who have lives to purify, may they feel purified

RELATION: MUSUBI

Leader   Think of ourselves as purified and restored to our potential

Think of us once again bound to nature and to the world around us in new and meaningful divine relation

Think of us as truly part of Great Nature

All   The power and purifying energy of nature, we will revere

The kami of heaven and earth, we will revere

CELEBRATION: MATSURI

Leader   Be thankful and be filled with the joy of life

Be thankful for what the wind and the lightning have taught you about life

Celebrate your purification

Rejoice in your enlightenment

All   We sing out our gratitude to the kami of heaven and earth

We celebrate in communion with the kami of heaven and earth and with those around us

WINTER

FUYU

WINTER

Fire

Fire in Religious Rituals

Fire has had its place in many religious traditions, whether as a symbol or even a deity itself. The fiery cross was used to rally the Celtic clans to battle in ages past. The fire altars of the Vikings (commemorated in the symbol of the Olympic flame) were the original symbols of Indra before the climatic factor changed Indra from being a deity of fire to being a deity of water. The reverence for flames inspired African tribes, ancient Egyptians, and Native Americans to use fire in their rituals. The Persians were famed worshipers of fire, and this has been carried into other Middle Eastern traditions. The Hebrew priest Samuel's duties included lighting the lamp in the temple, the sacred flame known as "the Lamp of God."

The Celtic Druids regarded fire with special understanding.

Fire was sacred in their temples and holy places to the extent that even trampling upon ashes was considered sacrilege. Perpetual fires were maintained by the virgin daughters of fire who were known as Breochwigh, the Keepers of the Sacred Fire. Bonfires were lit in Christian Celtic times to purify the air of hobgoblins and foul fiends. On the Vigil of St. John every year, long torches (like the *taima* in some Shinto festivals) are lit and carried through the streets in order to purify them from things that would harm people. In Celtic Christian homes, there were prayers for ancestors to be spoken as the household fire was lit in the morning.

Fire in Shinto

Fire is viewed ambiguously in Shinto. It was by giving birth to the kami of fire that Izanami died, leading her partner Izanagi to recognize the great and terrifying powers the kami of fire possessed. Fire can heat, but it can also destroy. Shinto undertook to subdue the dangerous aspects of fire. Fire-walking in Shinto rituals is practiced to assist the individual in his or her efforts to transcend the power of fire to inflict damage or pain.

This litany tries to gather together these many insights about fire into a composite liturgy that expresses the human dependence upon fire as well as the need for humans to control its wild character.

The Litany of Fire

OBSERVATION: KANNAGARA

Leader   Let us consider the nature of the divine, Nature the Mother and Nature the Father, the destructive and the purifying power of fire

Let us think of the self-disclosure of the divine in the providence and power of nature

Let us think of the fire as a dancing concentration of beauty, power, and energy united in endlessly renewing flow

All   Our senses have been dulled and dimmed, and we see nature not as the environment of our life, but as a tool to be used

Our senses are blind to its mystery and meaning

Our senses need the purification that will enable us to see nature as our teacher and guide

INVOCATION: DAISHIZEN

Leader   In the heat of the fire, all impurity is purged and taken away

The flames consume those things that we neither need nor want

All   Great Fire, speak to us and teach us your wisdom

In opening ourselves to nature, in seeking its purification, and in hearing what it has to teach us, may we find enlightenment as we share in the fusion of ourselves with the universe that brings us back to the divine that is within the human

INSPIRATION: KAMI

Leader   Speak to us of the flow of life as the fire that grows and consumes, and not as completion, not as alpha and omega, but as the beginning that never ends and the end that never ceases—the flame that always burns but is never consumed

Speak to us of the meaning of change, purification, and the communion of elements within the process of becoming eternally new

All   Teach us the meaning of purity, brightness, and the uprightness of the soul

Teach us how to return to our higher origins

Teach us the power of purification

PURIFICATION: HARAI

Leader   Let us repeat the words of the *Rokkon-shojo* with careful minds

All   Although the impure and polluted appears before my eyes, I will not let it blind me

Although it strikes my ears, I will not let it make me deaf

Although my nose senses it, I will not let it deform my soul

Although it enters my mouth, I will not let it destroy my taste for life

Although it touches my body, I will not let it cling to me

Although I may even desire it, I will not let that desire dwell within me

[Pause in silence]

Purified, we become free

Purified, our eyes are opened to the beauty and glory of nature

Purified, our ears can hear the harmony of the spheres even amid the discord of life

Purified, our sense of fragrance and spirituality is heightened

Purified, our taste can savor the subtle richness of life

Purified, our hands can touch the world in its strength and delicacy

Purified, our minds see and grasp the world as it is

Through these means, we will magnify the purity of our spirits and seek the divine within the human

MEDITATION: CHINKON

Leader Think on these things

The cleansing flame that consumes impurities like the divine that never dies

The form changeless yet ever-changing that can teach us the power of renewal

The divine within the cosmos and the divine within us

All: Those who have eyes that wish to see, may they see

Those who have spirits they seek to stir, may they feel stirred

Those who have lives to purify, may they feel purified

RELATION: MUSUBI

Leader Think of ourselves as purified and restored to our potential

Think of us once again bound to nature and to the world around us in new and meaningful divine relation

Think of us as truly part of Great Nature

All The power and purifying energy of fire and of nature, we will revere

The kami of heaven and earth, we will revere

CELEBRATION: MATSURI

Leader Be thankful and be filled with the joy of life

Be thankful for what fire has taught you about life

Celebrate your purification

Rejoice in your enlightenment

All We sing out our gratitude to the kami of heaven and earth

We celebrate in communion with the kami of heaven and earth and with those around us

Mountains

Mountains in Religion

Mountains have a special place in religious thought not simply because they lift people nearer heaven, but because they are sacred places in their own right.

It was on Mt. Sinai that the Ten Commandments were delivered to Moses on two tablets of stone. Isaiah predicted the Holy Mountain would arise above all other mountains in latter days. Mt. Zion became a symbol of the apocalyptic dream that enabled the spiritual hopes of the Judeo-Christian tradition to look ahead and seek its golden age of tomorrow.

The Celtic Druids of Ireland had the sacred hill of Tara, the high civilization of the ancient cult that was celebrated in song and poetic words. The king lived there, above yet with the people, simultaneously transcendent and immanent, invisible yet very visible. The Confucian view of mountains in China was that they were the place of the good man: "the wise man loves the sea, the good man loves the mountains."

Mountains in Japanese Religion

Mt. Fuji, the world's tallest volcano, was in the past acknowledged as a kami itself and will always be considered a place where kami could reside. The ancient Japanese celebrated it in the poetry of the *Man'yoshu*, Japan's oldest collection of poems. Of particular interest are the poems that describe the awesome power of Mt. Fuji, which obviously was very much active at the time of the composition of the poems in its honor. (The last eruption was in 1707.) The sight of that great mountain belching smoke and fire must have been indeed awesome. Judging by the accounts given, the melting snows were enough to make a river for people to use for transport, while birds were afraid to fly past the crater. It is hardly surprising that the Japanese sense of kami grew out of such a sense of reverence at nature's impressive and majestic powers.

Kami of the Mountains

Mountaineering may have become a Western hobby, but centuries before, it was a Japanese discipline of purification. *Sen-nichi-kai-ho-gyo*, the discipline of the Tendai monks running one thousand days around the peaks of Mt. Hiei in Kyoto, was designed to extend and enrich the human capacities. In the Kumano region, the Omine range of mountains was popular with ancient Japanese ascetics who purified themselves in the waterfalls and lived in seclusion to cultivate special powers. The famous blind shamans who convey the voices of the dead to the living work on Mt. Osore. Nichiren, Japan's most vigorous and fiery Buddhist leader of the Kamakura period, found enlightenment watching the sunrise from a mountaintop.

A sense of the power of the universe can be found on mountaintops by those who seek it. This litany incorporates many of these themes in honor of the mountain as a religious symbol.

The Litany of the Mountain

OBSERVATION: KANNAGARA

Leader Think of a mountain toward which you have a special feeling

Think of the idea of ascent for purification and enlightenment to a sacred place for communion with the divine

Let us think of the self-disclosure of the divine in the providence and power of nature

Let us think of the mountain as a concentration of beauty, power, and energy united in endless endurance

Think of how it remains unchanged yet changes its mantle with the seasons

Think of it as the home of life, the source of the river, and the shelter from the winds

All   Our senses have been dulled and dimmed, and we see nature not as the environment of our life, but as a tool to be used

Our senses are blind to its mystery and meaning

Our senses need the purification that will enable us to see nature as our teacher and guide

INVOCATION: DAISHIZEN

Leader   On the peak of the mountain, in the coldness and stark bareness of the rocks, can be purity and freedom

In the flow of the melting snows, all impurity is removed and washed away

The flow of life carries away those things that we neither need nor want

All   Great Mountain, speak to us and teach us your wisdom

Speak to us of the heights of life to be scaled as growth and not completion

In opening ourselves to nature, in seeking its purification, and in hearing what it has to teach us, may we find enlightenment as we share in the fusion of ourselves with the universe that brings us back to the divine that is within the human

INSPIRATION: KAMI

Leader   Speak to us of the strength and the endurance of the mountains, not as alpha and omega, but as the beginning that never ends and the end that never ceases—from their volcanic roots to their hardened peaks

Speak to us of the meaning of change, purification, and the communion of elements within the process of becoming eternally new

Enrich our perception of the highest possibility within this amazing universe of which we are a part

All   Teach us the meaning of purity, brightness, and the uprightness of the soul

Teach us how to return to our higher origins

Teach us the power of purification

PURIFICATION: HARAI

Leader   Let us repeat the words of the *Rokkon-shojo* with careful minds

All   Although the impure and polluted appears before my eyes, I will not let it blind me

Although it strikes my ears, I will not let it make me deaf

Although my nose senses it, I will not let it deform my soul

Although it enters my mouth, I will not let it destroy my taste for life

Although it touches my body, I will not let it cling to me

Although I may even desire it, I will not let that desire dwell within me

[Pause in silence]

Purified, we become free

Purified, our eyes are opened to the beauty and glory of nature

Purified, our ears can hear the harmony of the spheres even amid the discord of life

Purified, our sense of fragrance and spirituality is heightened

Purified, our taste can savor the subtle richness of life

Purified, our hands can touch the world in its strength and delicacy

Purified, our minds see and grasp the world as it is

Through these means, we will magnify the purity of our spirits and seek the divine within the human

MEDITATION: CHINKON

Leader   Think on these things

The flow that never ceases, the divine that never dies

The form changeless yet ever-changing that can grant us the power of renewal

The divine within the cosmos and the divine within us

All Those who have eyes that wish to see, may they see

Those who have spirits they seek to stir, may they feel stirred

Those who have lives to purify, may they feel purified

RELATION: MUSUBI

Leader Think of ourselves as purified and restored to our potential

Think of us once again bound to nature and to the world around us in new and meaningful divine relation

Think of us as truly part of Great Nature

All The power and purifying energy of nature, we will revere

The kami of heaven and earth, we will revere

CELEBRATION: MATSURI

Leader Be thankful and be filled with the joy of life

Be thankful for what the mountain has taught you about life

Celebrate your purification

Rejoice in your enlightenment

All We sing out our gratitude to the kami of heaven and earth

We celebrate in communion with the kami of heaven and earth and with those around us

Misogi:
Waterfall Purification

People seeking to be close to the kami should work at showing cleanness, brightness, and diligence in all that they do. Misogi regularly practiced can help. —YUKITAKA YAMAMOTO

Religion in modern society is studied from the viewpoint of economics, sociology, politics, philosophy, and psychology. Surely alongside these it is also fair to look at religion from the point of view of religion itself. From this perspective, we can speak of Shinto as one way of affirming the mysterious in the face of attitudes and beliefs that deny mystery in favor of "explicit rational proof."

Shinto and the Intuitive Awareness of the Mysterious

Acceptance of the mysterious is the recognition of knowledge beyond knowledge. There are the things we know, and there are the things we do not know. There are also things that, when the technology arrives, we can eventually know. But there is also knowledge beyond our understanding, the knowledge that is impossible to know because of the constitution of the human mind. We may know that a certain phenomenon exists, but not what it is. This is the core of the mysterious, the magnetic origins of faith.

Western and Japanese Asceticism

Ascetics live at the heart of their spiritual energy, and therefore their actions and responses may perhaps seem exaggerated. This is certainly true of some kinds of asceticism that have shown the tendency to go to extremes. Ascetics have grasped a way and travel along that way as far as possible, to the point of the extinction of the self in some cases. From ascetics, we can learn the way to the deep metaphysics of inner experience. We need not go so far as ascetics, but once we venture along their path, we can have a different perspective.

Western Asceticism itself offers little to attract great followings, mainly because of its history. Its vicious dualism of body and soul was designed to punish the body in order to save the soul. The medieval hair shirts, burrs in the shoes, self-flagellation, and other forms of punishment and self-abnegation have given to it an air of the morose, and even the masochistic. Its practices betrayed a gloomy view of humanity and an equally negative view of the divine.

Japanese ascetics, by contrast, seek to enhance human powers, to find renewal through the rituals and the discipline. There is nothing negative about their goals. There may be solemn ceremonies, but these generate energy and induce lightness of heart. These effects arise from heightened awareness of the natu-

Group misogi is not customary in Japan, where it is usually practiced in the sea or in lakes or rivers. But it may well be a suitable adaptation in the West. Here are members of the Wago Enten aikido dojo practicing group misogi at Manoa Waterfalls in Honolulu, Hawaii.

ral and the cosmic that reminds humans of the ultimate context of their existence.

What Is Misogi?

Misogi is the generic form of the Shinto act of purification. It can be traced back to when Izanagi left the land of impurity and bathed himself in the Tachibana River. The response of Japanese culture to all of life's "boundary situations," as existentialists have called them, is purification to seek renewal. It can be performed in the sea, in a river, or under a free-flowing waterfall. The form we will discuss here is waterfall purification because it is dynamic and profoundly inspirational to those who have performed it. Its purpose is to commune with the kami of the falls, to be united with nature, to touch the cosmos, and to seek renewal through cleansing

Misogi seems a simple act, but if we examine its various features, we can see where its power, attraction, and efficacy can be found, and why for countless centuries Japanese have gone to the mountains to perform this ritual. Let me offer four simple comments that will add some substance to these observations.

A BASIC FORM OF PURE EXPERIENCE

There is ultimate authenticity in the act of standing under the falls and being immersed in nature itself. You will not know where your physical existence ends and the flow of the falls begins. For that moment, you and nature are one. Misogi simultaneously creates the awareness and satisfies the longing of the spiritual hungry to feel and experience nature in a way that affirms our roots. Standing under the falls, we are a part of nature's process for that time, an indistinguishable element of it, returning to the source of life.

Today's world is short on opportunities for primal experience. The growing fascination, almost obsession with cyberspace and its potential has given us virtual reality, virtual sex, virtual churches, in a word, virtual experience. People learn from others what an experience is supposed to be, or should be. Experiences then come to be measured by what others say, by what they report, or by what so-called experts claim. Misogi is one way back to the discovery of pure experience and to the search for authenticity.

RENEWAL THROUGH REPETITION

Nowhere is the power to be born again and again more effectively demonstrated than in the ritual of misogi. Individual needs and group purposes can be met, in time, through repetition of this rite. It is not a once and only, absolute experience. Repetition heightens the quality and awakens the realization that life is not a state of being, but a flowing, vital, and active process.

Over the years I have practiced misogi myself, I have led many groups of students and businesspeople, more Westerners than Japanese, in undergoing the experience. Never in those years have people failed to find the experience stimulating and inspiring. Many have made the great effort to come back not just once but as often as circumstances would permit. They have begun to discover the meaning of renewal and wanted to travel again on that road. They have come to realize that the search for enlightenment should be accompanied by the pursuit of renewal as a holistic undertaking.

A PROFOUND DISCIPLINE OF THE SPIRIT

The power of misogi to renew comes from its being a discipline of the human spirit. My good friend, fellow pilgrim, and High Priest of the Tsubaki Grand Shrine, the Reverend Yukitaka Yamamoto, in response to his own basic yearning, performed misogi every midnight for ten years to discover the meaning of spirituality that had led to his total renewal. Meeting him, you would see at once from the vitality within him that he is in every sense reborn, a model of what human life is capable of reaching.

For people who seek to change the patterns of life or to deepen and discover meaning, misogi has provided the energizing resources by training the soul. The repetition and the discipline make steady renewal possible as a form of personal growth and development. It is indeed on a par with a physical training of an athlete. It is the holistic, psychophysical training of a spiritual athlete. Japan's ascetics are Olympians of the spiritual world. They are the pioneers and discoverers of the vast tracts of uncharted inner life that leads to outer change and renewal. They are bearers and practitioners of one of life's greatest secrets.

COSMIC AWARENESS

Misogi possesses the power to generate the cosmic awareness that I have suggested is tragically missing from modern life. The power of the cosmos is released in misogi. In the experience, for a split second, anyone can visit the infinity of the outer domains of space in their own existence. By transcending time and space, motion or place, the locus of humanity within the great cosmic configuration of power and energy is confirmed. Awareness of quality and possibility thus becomes heightened. This is a kind of instant enlightenment. Of course it is too brief an encounter for any articulation to take place; therefore you must repeat misogi to become familiar with the sense of the cosmic and to feel at home and natural within it.

How to Perform Misogi

As I stated earlier, misogi may be performed in a variety of ways in different sources of water. In some cases, as with my Scottish friend Mari whose story I told in the preface, it's possible to practice this ritual without being aware of its name or origin. In the following, I want to take you through the experience of misogi as it is performed at the Tsubaki Grand Shrine. But I want to emphasize that you can perform misogi yourself, wherever you like, without necessarily employing the customary preparations and rituals.

Before misogi, the mind and body should be conditioned. The night before, you should try to avoid meat and alcohol. Your senses will be freed and made readily receptive if you shun any physical substances that might cloud or distort them.

Preparation for those taking part at Tsubaki Grand Shrine begins when they assemble in front of the shrine office at the agreed time and from there proceed into the hall beside the *haiden* (shrine sanctuary) to receive a simplified form of harai called *shubatsu*. The waterfall is a kami, so there is need for purification before entering it. In the dressing rooms, men don white loincloths and *hachimaki* (headbands). Women also wear hachimaki in addition to long white kimono. After coming out of the dressing areas, they move down to an open area above the entrance to the waterfall and face the *honden* (main shrine). They bow twice, clap twice, then bow once more.

The participants are now ready to commence the warm-up exercises.

If you are without benefit of a trained leader (*michihiko*), you can prepare for misogi by sitting quietly near the the falls, meditating and relaxing for several minutes before approaching the base of the falls. Bowing and clapping are important parts of this any many other Shinto rituals. Bowing shows respect and gratitude. The clap, like ringing the bell at a Shinto shrine, announces your presence to the kami and also balances and purifies the energy flow of nature. Always raise your hands to chest height and clap sharply palm to palm.

Exercises 1–5 are traditional warm-up exercises designed to condition you to enter the falls. They can be conducted just at the water's edge. Throughout some phrases are given in Japanese and English. You can use whichever form you prefer.

EXERCISE 1: FURITAMA ("SOUL SHAKING")

1. Stand up straight with your legs apart about shoulder width.

2. Place your right hand over the left in front of your lower abdomen, leaving a space between your hands the size of a ping-pong ball.

3. Shake your hands vigorously up and down.

4. While shaking your hands, concentrate and repeat the following words, which are an invocation to the kami of the place of purification:

   Harae-do-no-Okami
   ("Kami of the place of purification, please purify our surroundings")

The object of Exercise 1 is to generate an awareness of the

soul within yourself. In Shinto, *kon* (the soul) is one of the four important elements, along with *mei* (life), *rei* (spirit), and *ki* (spiritual energy). Kon is the most important of the four since human beings can also be described as *waketama* (individual souls), which is another way of saying "children of the kami."

EXERCISE 2: TORIFUNE ("A BIRD ROWING")

1. Stand up straight and put your left leg forward.

2. Clench both fists with your thumbs tucked inside your rolled fingers.

3. Lean forward. Starting from above your left knee and ending back near your armpits, pump both your arms as though rowing a boat. As you "row," shout, *"Yie!"*

4. Perform this twenty times, then repeat Furitama (Exercise 1).

5. Repeat Torifune, this time with your right leg forward, shouting, *"Ei!"* and *"Ho!"* alternately. Do this twenty times, then repeat Furitama.

6. Return to a stance with your left foot forward and bring your clenched fists up to your chest with a shout *"Yie!"* Thrust your hands down and forward, opening your hands and extending your fingers to a shout of *"Sa!"*

7. Once again repeat Furitama.

Exercise 2 introduces a dimension of physical calisthenics to go along with the spiritual training. Since misogi is a holistic body/mind experience, both types of warm-up are necessary.

EXERCISE 3: OTAKEBI ("VOCALIZATION")

1. Stand up straight with your feet slightly apart.

2. Place your hands on your hips.

3. Follow the michihiko in shouting the following three invocations:

   Iku-tama! Taru-tama! Tama-tamaru-tama!

4. Follow the michihiko by repeating three times the longer invocation:

   Okami! Okami! Kunitsu-Okami! Sarutahiko Okami To-toshi-ya!
   (Kami! Kami! Kami of the earth! Great and Glorious Sarutahiko, Head of the kami of earth!)

The object of Exercise 3 is threefold. Shouting, *Iku-tama* activates the soul to awareness. *Taru-tama* affirms the awareness that you can realize the infinite in your soul. *Tama-tamaru-tama* confirms both previous invocations and keeps the soul activated. The closing invocation addresses and acknowledges the power of Sarutahiko Okami, head of the earthly kami.

EXERCISE 4: OKOROBI ("YIELDING")

1. Stand up straight with your feet slightly apart.

2. Place your left hand on your hip and hold your right hand to your forehead with two fingers extended in a gesture that resembles the Boy Scout salute.

3. With your right hand, cut the air in a sweeping gesture downward from right to left as you invoke each kami by name:

Kunitoko-tachi-no-Mikoto! Yie!

Sarutahiko-no-Okami! Yie!

Kokuryu-no-Okami! Yie!

4. With each gesture, step forward with your left foot and then step back again.

Exercise 4 invokes three important kami: Kunitoko-tachi-no-Mikoto (the earthly kami), Sarutahiko-no-Okami (the kami of guidance and head of the earthly kami), and Kokuryu-no-Okami (the kami of water, life, and ki). This allows you to unite with them, receive their power, and have your impurities removed.

EXERCISE 5: IBUKI ("BREATHING")

1. Stand up straight with your feet slightly apart.

2. Lower your hands and arms toward your knees with your palms slightly upward and outward.

3. Begin a slow inhale as you extend your arms fully outward to each side and lift them above your head until your palms and fingers meet.

4. Begin a slow exhale and, keeping your palms and fingers together, bring your hands straight down in front of you until you have a prayerlike Buddha-hand shape just below your navel. Pause there slightly.

5. Now continue to bring your hands and arms back down to your sides as you finish exhaling.

6. Repeat the entire sequence five times.

7. Turn to face the waterfall, bow twice, clap twice sharply, and open your arms palms upward toward the falls.

Exercise 5 concludes your preparations. By taking deep breaths you absorb the ki of the cosmos and raise the metabolism of the ki to its highest level of sensitivity and receptivity.

EXERCISE 6: NYUSUI ("ENTERING THE WATER")

1. Just before you enter the water, the michihiko sprinkles *sakashio* (purifying salt) on you.

2. The michihiko hands you a ladle of salted Japanese sake; take the liquid into your mouth and spray it in three mouthfuls into the stream.

3. The michihiko recites the nine-character prayer as follows:

   Rin-pyo-to-sha-kai-zin-retsu-zai-zen.

4. The michihiko then cuts the air symbolically nine times shouting, "*Yie!*"

5. Enter the area by the falls and splash water on your face, chest, and loins.

6. Clap your hands twice sharply and bow once toward the waterfall.

7. With your right hand, cut the air from right to left as in Exercise 4.

8. Approach the waterfall and enter it, right shoulder first. Turn around and face the michihiko, holding your

hands clasped in front with your middle fingers together and pointing away from you.

9. Shout the following words:

Harae-tamae, kiyome-tamae, Rokkon-shojo!
("Purify my soul, wash my soul, purify the six body
zones where impurities can enter")

Continue until the Michihiko shouts, *"Yie!"* as a signal to
come out.

10. Withdraw from the falls. Once you are out of the water,
clap your hands sharply twice and bow once as you
face the falls.

In step 3 the sequence from one to nine is invoked to
symbolize the secular world and its impurities. Using a cutting
gesture before entering the water in step 4 implies the removal of
impurities from the nine areas of existence. The expressions *harae*
and *kiyome* in step 9 ask for the purifying of the individual by the
washing away of all impurities from the six elements of human
beings that Shinto identifies—the five senses and the mind. The
Rokkon-shojo invocation from Tsubaki Grand Shrine, which was
adapted for this book's meditation litanies on nature, refers to
each of the elements in turn:

> Although the impure and polluted appears before my eyes, I will
> not let it blind me. Although it strikes my ears, I will not let it
> make me deaf. Although my nose senses it, I will not let it de-
> form my soul. Although it enters my mouth, I will not let it de-
> stroy my taste for life. Although it touches my body, I will not let
> it cling to me. Although I may even desire it, I will not let that de-
> sire dwell within me.

CHINKON: MEDITATION

After drying off, participants return to the haiden for a period of chinkon to pacify the soul. This in turn is followed by a *naorai*, a ritual drinking with the kami that has the effect of strengthening the vertical musubi, that is, the connection between people and kami. This is also a celebration among people, so the horizontal musubi, the connection among participants, also becomes stronger.

Misogi is physically as well as spiritually therapeutic. The impact of the waterfall on the back of the neck removes stress stored in the muscles there. On one occasion, we checked the blood pressure of several participants before misogi, immediately after the ritual, and about thirty minutes into chinkon. Following an expected immediate rise, everyone showed a marked lowering from the pre-misogi level after half an hour. This suggests that it has some effect in stress reduction and may indirectly contribute to the improvement of health and longevity.

Misogi in the style of Tsubaki Grand Shrine has been practiced for centuries. There is good reason to believe that people in ages past knew more of the secrets of nature than we know in our modern state of alienation from nature. I wish that I could explain all of Great Nature's mysteries, but my own experiences with misogi convince me of its power to do many good things for those who are receptive to its healing and renewing power.

Shinto in North America

Shinto . . . can freely meet and mix with any tradition that seeks for the highest in humankind to be infused with the finest that the divine can inspire in it. —YUKITAKA YAMAMOTO

North America boasts almost every religion under the sun, and some that are hard to find elsewhere. In the wide open spaces of the American plains, in the vastness of the great mountains and valleys, there has been room over the past three centuries for almost every type of spiritual plant to take root. From Abraham to Zoroaster, from Armenian Christianity to Zen Buddhism, spiritual gurus and historical cults have grown and flourished. In recent times, to that impressive list has been added the name of Shinto from Japan. How did that come about?

North America Welcomes Shinto

Who would have imagined that a religious tradition singled out by the U.S. propaganda machine during World War II for vilification could find welcome on American soil? But then who would have predicted twenty years ago that New York sirloin steak lovers

would turn with ease to sushi bars to help balance their choles-
terol? Many strange turns of fate are beyond explanation. This
one, however, is not.

The arrival of Shinto in North America has nothing to do
with Japanese imperialism. The "Yellow Peril" is, and always has
been, a psychotic and neurotic myth of frightened people. Nor is
Shinto's emergence the result of Japanese immigrants and their
children, many of whom suffered in wartime internment camps.
Nor was it slick marketing. In that area, Shinto shrines possess
varying skills, from little to none whatsoever.

Oddly enough, it was not a Japanese initiative toward
North America. It was the other way round.

Perceptive souls from North America, possessed of a
broad and enriched sense of religious potential, were able to see
in Shinto a primeval view of human spirituality and life that had
the capacity to become a New Wave of the future. Tired of dogma
and spiritual dictatorships, they found in the simple but basic
practices of Shinto something that called them back to roots that
they had forgotten. At the beginning they did not know its name
or even understand what the priests were saying. But it inspired
them, and they listened to its call. Let me illustrate.

In the Heart of Mt. Tamalpais

I have a wonderful memory of a most amazing event that took
place near San Francisco, deep in the heart of Mt. Tamalpais just
north of the Golden Gate. That mountain is still a sacred place to

Native Americans, and to anyone who can sense the sound of silence, it was well designated a dwelling place of the great spirit.

We were a strange company that day. As I recollect, there were two Shinto priests, a Scottish Presbyterian cleric, two Unitarian ministers, and a wonderful family. The father was an Austrian-born gentleman with an American wife. They had a beautiful little baby, who had, as babies can do, imparted to his father a vision of spiritual rebirth. The man had been born into a rigid Roman Catholic family in Austria and had had his fill of dogma. He had come to America to capitalize on the American Dream and was one of the lucky ones. But after a successful business life, having a wonderful little baby boy when he was almost eighty years of age made him feel as though his rebirth was not complete. He wanted to find something simple but deeply satisfying. He had joined a Unitarian Fellowship and wanted a memorable initiation. Someone had told him about Shinto and purification, and he initiated contact. Plans were made, dates fixed, and on a warm spring day, we set off on a long spiritual pilgrimage into the heart of the mountain to find a place for peace, purification, and spiritual empowerment.

I guess we may have walked for an hour and a half, slowly and carefully, when we found a location that, before we saw it, called to us. A little creek beckoned. The water ran down through an archway of rocks, forming a covered waterfall. Nature had created it, and nature was pointing out to us that this was the place. To the spiritual mountaineers of Tibet and the esoteric Buddhist/Shinto ascetics of Japan, such a place is immediately recognizable because of the power it emanates. Here was a source of purification and energy, set in an idyllic atmosphere of peace and tranquility. It found us, as it probably had thousands in past millennia. We merely happened upon it.

Having agreed, with hardly a word exchanged, and using the rudimentary cover that nature provided, we undressed and prepared for misogi. I will not go into the details of the event, but I invite you to imagine the implicit universality of this scenario in which such diverse people could follow nature, follow the prompting of the mountain, and eventually experience a power surge in spirituality that left every single participant breathless and inspired. I will never forget the joy on that man's face as he completed the ritual and declared that now his life had truly both begun and been fulfilled at the same time—just like my Scottish friend in the preface. Neither of them had found Shinto. In nature, Shinto had called to them. It had not said, "Believe this, trust that." It had said simply, "Do this, and rejoice in life!" All of us did, and the memory lingers.

Buddhism Immigrates to the U.S.A.

Shinto is not as well known in the United States as Buddhism. Buddhism in America has been the theme of conferences, symposia, anthologies, and college classes for many years. Since Daisetsu Suzuki popularized Zen in the early 1960s, Buddhism has gained a small but steadily growing following. Some of Hollywood's VIPs profess some kind of Buddhist philosophy, and Buddhist communities may be found in many parts of the continental U.S., notably in California. This is the result not only of

Americans' interest in Buddhism but also of Japanese immigration to the U.S. during the Meiji period (1868–1912), a time when Japan was setting out on the road to modernization. You will find Buddhist temples everywhere Japanese emigrated at that time, from Brazil to Canada, but Shinto shrines remain a rarity. Why?

One reason is that Buddhism is heavily concerned with death, redesigned as it was in both China and Japan to meet the needs of cultures steeped in ancestral reverence.

Death rituals are very important for Japanese. Therefore it is significant that while the local American population became enamored with Zen, Japanese immigrants retained their more popular Jodo Shin, or True Pure Land, Buddhist tradition. In Japan, Zen, in numerical terms of temples and followers, is very much a minority tradition of Buddhism, albeit an important minority. Jodo Shin accounts for almost half of all Buddhist temples in the country. It is not surprising that immigrants should take with them the rituals that would pacify and revere the souls of their departed relatives in a proper manner. In Japanese culture, souls not pacified can be troublesome, and a special ritual is often required to remove the causes of distress.

Shinto, by contrast, was much more difficult to export for several reasons. One reason is that Shinto was developed from elements indigenous to the Japanese islands. The shrines weren't just places to worship built wherever it was convenient but were special sites linked to the natural landscape where the kami interacted with humans. For emigrating Japanese, finding such sacred spots in a new land may have seemed improbable. As a religion, Buddhism is far more organized than Shinto, which had no known human originator, lacked well-defined orthodoxy, and de-

Kamisama Shinzo (statue) and torii *on the grounds of Tsubaki Grand Shrine of America. On the right is where worshipers hang votive* ema *plaques.*

veloped almost as a group of cults dedicated to the local kami of each particular region. One more reason for the advantage Buddhism enjoys in North America is the U.S. wartime propaganda that focused on State Shinto as a cause of the Pacific War and has influenced popular Western images of this religion ever since.

Postwar Shinto Shrines in North America

Considering Shinto's unfortunate negative reputation in the U.S., it was a brave act when High Priest Yukitaka Yamamoto set out for New York to perform a Shinto ritual in the UN Plaza for the success of the Apollo 9 moon landing in 1969. Feeling little hostility toward him subsequently, and believing in the importance of enriching links between Japan and its former enemy and occupier, Dr. Yamamoto (who kindly provided the foreword to this book) fulfilled a dream by establishing Tsubaki Grand Shrine of America in Stockton, California, in 1987 as a point of meeting and exchange between his native land and the United States.

Following this groundbreaking event was the establishment in the Seattle area of Tsubaki Kannagara Jinja in 1992. A third branch of Tsubaki Grand Shrine in North America was set up in Vancouver, British Columbia, in the spring of 1998 to assist in promoting the cultural exchange goals of Tsubaki Grand Shrine of America.

For a number of reasons, including a generous donation of land in Seattle next to Tsubaki Kannagara Jinja, Tsubaki Grand Shrine of America was transported to Seattle in 2001. Rev. Koichi Barrish, the Guji (chief priest), is the first American to become a licensed Shrine Shinto priest. He is the shrine director and Senior Priest of Tsubaki Grand Shrine of America. You can visit the shrine and participate in ceremonies like misogi as well as rituals and celebrations throughout the year. The shrine welcomes inquiries about Shinto from interested parties. It publishes a newsletter in English and operates its own web site at www.tsubakishrine.com.

> Tsubaki Grand Shrine of America and
> Tsubaki Kannagara Jinja
> 17720 Crooked Mile Road
> Granite Falls, WA 98252
> Tel. (360) 691-6389
> Kannushi@TsubakiShrine.com
> www.tsubakishrine.com

Other Shinto Shrines outside Japan

Both Hawaii and Brazil are host to large shrines. These two shrines were the work of immigrants rather than missionaries. Indeed, the idea of a missionary in the Western sense of a proselytizer is totally alien to Shinto. In Honolulu is a branch of the famous Izumo Taisha shrine of Japan, a shrine referred to in Japanese mythology as the great eight-fathom palace of Izumo.

> Hawaii Izumo Taisha
> 215 North Kukui Street
> Honolulu, Hawaii 96817
> Tel: (808) 538-7778

In Brazil, the shrine is known as Brasil Dai Jingu, or the Great Imperial shrine of Brazil:

> Brasil Dai Jingu
> Estrada De Santa Isabel, KM40.5
> CX Postal 54CEP 07400, Aruja-Estado
> Sao Paulo, Brazil
> Tel: (011) 466-0759

Shinto Transcends Boundaries and Borders

I have one last event in mind, comic rather than cosmic, that nevertheless demonstrates both the power of misogi and the concept that Shinto is not alien to American soil or water. Sometime during the mid-1980s, Dr. Yamamoto and the head of the International Division of Tsubaki Grand Shrine of America accompanied me to Sacramento, where we rented a car and drove to our destination at a national park about two hours north into the mountains. Our goal was to find a waterfall, recommended to us, where we could perform misogi during a summer conference.

We found the park, but no rangers were in sight, so we walked for about half an hour before finding the falls. It was awesome—about 100 feet wide with a 60-foot drop. To the right was a broken tree over which the waters were cascading toward the rocks below. A quick conference decided that I would go up and hold on to the tree branches and try to "say the words." The High Priest chanted the proper form as I felt the force of water falling from 60 feet hit the back of my neck. I thought I had myself become a power source, feeling as though I would light up any minute.

About halfway through, two strange things occurred simultaneously. First, my shorts were filling with water and were about to drop in sight of all. Second, as fate would have it, a park ranger appeared on the road above in a 4x4, and what I imagined as a he was a she. The water and gravity won, and I almost got arrested! The ranger told me she was impressed by my sense of balance in what she saw was a dangerous situation. I explained that my Shinto pals were in charge, and that it was OK by heaven. She was not too convinced.

As my Japanese friends were trying to impede my arrest, I prowled around looking for a challenge to my newfound hydro-electric power. You may have seen my fellow Scots tossing the caber, a telegraph-pole-sized tree trunk, at the many Highland Games around the world. The caber is a test of strength for "real men." I noticed a log that looked to be around 20 feet long and 9 inches in diameter and had the urge to raise it and toss it. I walked under it and stood it up. In the small clearing where I found it, I lifted the log onto my hips, ran with it, and tossed it into perfect position. The ranger came out and saw what I was doing. My friends were fascinated but not surprised. They knew about the power that misogi can generate. Finally, with a smile, she told my Japanese friends to take their monster friend home, and not to come back. Anyway, there was no water there in summer.

* * *

Human beings can find real power in nature, no matter in which country they happen to find themselves. How does Shinto look in North America? Not at all out of place. Why? Because most of the necessary awareness is already in place. It is just that perhaps Americans haven't yet found the words to express their respect for and appreciation of Great Nature. The U.S. and Japan are not the most similar of cultures and can have difficulty comprehending each other, but through Shinto, they can find closer understanding and communion of minds.

Shinto makes no claim to "universality," which can be an argument for absolutism or authoritarianism when used by organizations claiming to possess a monopoly on the truth. Rather, Shinto can *enrich* all religion with the same awareness of the universal found in prehistorical religious cultures that depend on nature as a guide and not upon doctrines of supernatural revelation.

I can only express the hope that those interested in the contents of this book will make contact with one of the groups I've mentioned to further the possibility of encountering Shinto, which is caught rather than taught. Encountering it live is much more illuminating than through the written word.

Glossary

ARAMITAMA: the wilder, destructive side of nature

CHINKON: a Shinto spiritual exercise

DAIJINJA: grand shrine

DAISHIZEN: "Great Nature," the cosmos

FURITAMA: "soul shaking," an exercise to prepare for misogi

HACHIMAKI: headband

HAIDEN: the outer worship hall of a shrine

HARAI: a Shinto ritual of purification

HONDEN: the main hall of a shrine

IBUKI: "breathing," an exercise to prepare for misogi

IZANAGI: the male kami who helped create then populate earth; he performed the first misogi to purify himself after returning from the land of pollution

IZANAMI: the female kami who helped create then populate the earth; she died giving birth to the kami of fire

JINJA: a Shinto shrine

KAMI, OKAMI: the deity or deities associated with a particular place or natural element

KANNAGARA: the movements, actions, and gestures that allow humans to live in the way of the kami

KI: "spiritual energy"

MATSURI: a festival or celebration

MEI: "life"

MICHIHIKO: the leader of a Shinto ritual

MISOGI: the Shinto ritual of purification in natural sources of water

MUSUBI: literally, "knot"; refers to the connection between people or between people and kami

NAORAI: ceremonial drinking with kami

NIGIMITAMA: the gentle, helpful side of nature

NORITO: an invocation to the kami

NYUSUI: "entering the water," an exercise to prepare for misogi

OKOROBI: "yielding," an exercise to prepare for misogi

OTAKEBI: "vocalization," an exercise to prepare for misogi

REI: "spirit"

ROKKON-SHOJO: a Shinto prayer said to purify the five senses and the mind during rituals

SARUTAHIKO OKAMI: the kami of guidance, head kami of earth

SHINBOKU: a tree designated as sacred by a thick, twisted rope attached around its trunk

TORIFUNE: "bird rowing," an exercise to prepare for misogi

TSUMI: impurity or wrongdoing, loosely analogous to the Western concept of sin, also including the sense of misfortune

ABOUT THE AUTHOR

Stuart D. B. Picken was educated at Allen Glen's School and the University of Glasgow, where he majored in philosophy and divinity. Ordained a Minister of the Church of Scotland in 1966, he served on the Faculty of International Christian University in Tokyo for twenty-five years prior to moving to Nagoya University of Commerce and Business Administration, where he has served as Dean of the Faculty of Foreign Languages and Asian Studies since its inception in 1998 and is Chairman of the Graduate School Division of Global Business Communication. His prior books include *Shinto: Japan's Spiritual Roots* (1979), *Buddhism: Japan's Cultural Identity*, and *Christianity and Japan: Meeting, Conflict, Hope*. He is also author of *The Essentials of Shinto* (1994) and *A Historical Dictionary of Shinto* (2002), as well as over two hundred academic papers and articles. From 1985 to 1988 he served as Director of the Center for Japanese Studies at the University of Stirling in Scotland and was instrumental in founding the Japan Society of Scotland. He has been actively involved in interreligious dialogues at many levels and in promoting the better understanding of Shinto and Japanese culture in international Asia and in the West. Since 1987 he has been International Advisor to the High Priest of Tsubaki Grand Shrine, Mie Prefecture, Japan.